Kingdom Movers

DIONNE RENEE

www.greatnesspublishing.org

Published by Greatness Publishing, Ontario, Canada

Cover Design by Akeem Brathwaite. Library and Archives Canada

ISBN 978-1-927579-56-5 (Electronic)

ISBN 978-1-927579-55-8 (Paperback)

ACKNOWLEDGMENTS

It is indeed a great honor and privilege to be used as an instrument for the Kingdom of God. My utmost prayer is that as you read this book and apply the wisdom gained, God will be able to experience you how He truly designed you to be.

Thank you, Holy Spirit! For it is you alone who deserves the glory. You are truly the author of this book, for it is you who gave the download of this revelation. I am just the vessel that was used to deliver this message. May people glorify you just as I am for this book.

I want to extend my thanks to my spiritual leaders, Drs. Andre and Nina Thomas who have been an inspiration for me. I so appreciate your leadership, mentorship, and guidance towards me. I thank God for gifting me two selfless people to direct me into His purpose for my life. I celebrate you both.

Thank you to my parents, Eric Brathwaite, and Pastor Hyacinth Brathwaite, for always encouraging and believing in me. You have always been a source of support and strength. I thank God for making you, my parents.

Thanks to Akeem Brathwaite, my kingdom brother, who did an amazing job with the book cover. You are indeed a great gift to the kingdom. You're always willing to assist the Kingdom of God with your artistic gifts. God bless you!

To Evangelist Cathy-Anne Forde, thank you! Truly, when God was creating persons that hold scribal and editorial giftings, I believe you were at the top of His list. Thanks once again for your encouragement and expertise in bringing this book together.

Finally, thank you to my family and loved ones who always show support and love throughout my God-given journey.

FOREWORD

It is apparent that the creator of life programmed movement in the gift of life. A sperm and an egg meet, and there is movement, a fetus is produced, and then there is movement. A child is formed in the womb, and then there is movement; the child is birthed, and then there are a series of movements that the child makes to reach adulthood. The child starts with nursery school, then primary school, secondary school, college, and the workforce.

This movement I have chronicled above is physical, but there is also spiritual movement. When a baby does not move from one form of growth to a higher form of growth, it's a sign that there is a problem that needs to be addressed. The same is true for the lack of spiritual movement. However, many people do not know how to read the signs, and if they do read the signs, they will not know what to do to move from stagnation into higher versions of themselves.

This book will give you a road map to help you identify where you are spiritually and the tools to help you move from one version of yourself to a higher version in the plans and purposes of God. Spiritual movement is not automatic; it must be initiated by the children of God.

My spiritual daughter Dionne has done a good job writing this book, and I believe it will be a blessing to many. Read well.

Ambassador Dr. Andre Thomas

TABLE OF CONTENTS

INTRODUCTION

We are God's offspring, made in His image & likeness, so naturally, we have aspects of God that are undeniable ***(Genesis 1:26).*** In His sovereignty, He has allowed us to possess His communicable attributes, one of which is His ability to move. God is a mover, and as His children, so are we! He moves to shift situations and people in place; He moves to order the steps of the righteous, and He orchestrates the seasons of time and chance for all.

As believers, we ought to comprehend that our spiritual lives move in accordance with God's Word and happenings. When He is ready to move in our lives, we must be prepared to be moved. **Acts 17:26 states, *"for in Him we live and move and have our being*** ....," so it stands to reason that God is the source of our very existence, strength, and movement. No longer can we think our prayer lives should be the same as when we were first saved, or it's okay to gloss over the Word of God once a week without even meditating on it and giving room for impartation from the Holy Spirit.

Meditating on the Word of God causes the spirit of that Word to enter our lives, resulting in the breakthrough, healing, deliverance, or miracle we need. We cannot stay stationary on the same level of worship year after year, just going to Sunday services, singing a couple of songs, and feeling encouraged when there's little or no intimacy, relationship, or fellowship with the Holy Spirit. We must understand that when we become more intimate with the Holy Spirit, He reveals what we need for our lives. In the Bible, we learn that we are children before we become sons, and in order to make that transition, a movement is required to achieve sonship.

Some of the definitions in Google's English dictionary for the word 'move' are:

- To go in a specified direction
- To make progress
- To change position
- To advance

As I meditated on these definitions, it brought me great insight. We must constantly move to align with God's agenda on the earth. We cannot stay still if we seek to operate in the spheres God has called us to. We cannot remain stuck in a location like the Israelites were in the wilderness if we want to be partakers of the fullness of His glory. We absolutely cannot stay in transit if we want to be a part of God's Wise Virgin Movement on the earth. You may wonder, what is God's Wise Virgin Movement?

In **Matthew 25**, we read about the story of the ten virgins who took their lamps and went to meet the bridegroom. Five of them were wise, and five were foolish. The five wise virgins took sufficient oil for their lamps, but the five foolish virgins did not take any oil with them and, as a result, ran out of oil when the bridegroom tarried. Consequently, they were left behind and unable to attend the marriage feast.

The Wise Virgin Movement is made up of believers whose lampstands are shining, and their lamps are full of oil. Wise Virgins are believers of Christ who allow their lights to shine before men so that they may glorify the Father of lights. These are the believers who do the works of destiny. They are not just churchgoers but destiny chasers. They bring solutions ordained by God to their generation and are relevant to their generation.

In order to possess, we have to make progress. ~Dionne Renee~

God's greatness is unsearchable. He is the infinite and omniscient God. There is no place big enough that can contain the fullness of God's presence. His agenda is so extraordinary that it takes generations to fulfill. The depth of His wisdom is incomprehensible. He is set apart from all else. He resides in a class all by Himself. I could not go any further unless I shared this imagery of how great God is and His agenda. Though it still does not do any justice nor encapsulate His supremacy in the least, it helps us understand the magnificence of God and that movement is required in the process for the works of God to be manifested. In preparation for us to progress, possess, and access the different dimensions of God so that we can establish the Kingdom of God here on earth, we cannot be motionless; for in Him, we move, so we must always be a people on the move. Life is lived in dimensions, and because God is a dimensional God, movement in the realm of the spirit is necessary to affect the movement in the realm of the natural.

This book brings revelation and wisdom of the importance of moving so that your light can shine in the sphere to which you are called. It highlights various biblical characters in their movement and alignment with God's agenda in their distinct assignments and purpose. I pray that as you read it, you will be inspired and motivated to recognize when God is moving and get into alignment with Him to facilitate your shining.

CHAPTER 1

Accessing Deeper Dimensions in God Requires Movement

To host a different dimension in God, you must keep moving because when you move, you align with a specific agenda. There must be a change of location spiritually and sometimes naturally. In the natural, you may be required to leave familiar places, things, and people. In this book, I will show you that although the people that I referenced made a physical move, a spiritual move first took place in their lives before it crystallized in the natural.

Abram's journey was a prominent example in the Bible, where movement was made evident. The journey was not only physical in nature, but it was also a spiritual move. For God to make him great, Abram had to leave his country, people, and father's household. His country and the people he associated with could not host the dimension of the blessing God was ready to pour out on him. It is necessary to understand that a shift must first take place in our spiritual coordinates to receive in the natural.

The Spirit realm will not release what the natural realm is not prepared to accommodate. **~Dionne Renee ~**

GOD told Abram, ***"Leave your country, your family, and your father's home for a land that I will show you. I'll make you a great nation and bless you. I'll make you famous; you'll be a blessing. I'll bless those who bless you; those who curse you I'll curse. All the families of the earth will be blessed through you" (Genesis 12: 1-3, Message).***

When I read the above verses, I wondered why God wanted Abram to leave his country and his father's home. Why did he have to move from his home? As I read the second verse, I understood the reason. God wanted to make him great. He wanted to do great things with Abram that his current environment would not permit. He wanted to bless him mightily – a blessing that would benefit all humankind. Abram's environment at the time was not conducive to what God wanted to do through and in him, hence his instruction to move. Human beings are gates, and God operates on the earth through man. Man is the gate that God utilizes to manifest His glory on the earth. (***Psalm 24:7 (NKJV): "Lift up your heads, O you gate! And be lifted up, you everlasting doors; and the King of glory shall come in"****).*

Genesis 1:26-28 (NKJV): "Then God said, "Let Us make man in Our image, according to Our likeness; let them have dominion over the fish of the sea, over the birds of the air, and over the cattle, over all the earth and over every creeping thing that creeps on the earth." So, God

created man in His own image; in the image of God He created him; male and female He created them. Then God blessed them, and God said to them, "Be fruitful and multiply; fill the earth and subdue it; have dominion over the fish of the sea, over the birds of the air, and over every living thing that moves on the earth."

As we see from the above scriptures, God can do nothing on the earth except He does it through mankind. God gave man complete dominion, authority, and power on the earth. Earth is man's domain to rule and reign, and if God wants to do something on the earth, it must come through the gate called 'man' because God is subject to His Word. Even though He is God and He owns everything, the rulership and control of the earth belong to man. He made it to be this way, and He is not a man that He should lie. Whatever His Word says, He backs and stands by it. It's even the same for the demonic; anything that the kingdom of darkness wants to establish on the earth has to be accomplished through the vessel of a man. It shows the kingdom of darkness is also subject to Heaven's rules and principles.

For God to express Himself and manifest His greatness and glory on the earth, He must do it through a man. It's why Jesus, even though He existed in Heaven before He came to earth, had to be born of a woman, become flesh, and become a man so God could get mankind back for Himself and give back the dominion to man that Satan had stolen in the Garden of Eden. He couldn't send an angel because it would go against the very protocol and principles of His Word. What Jesus did on the cross could have only been accomplished through a man; hence, Christ, the man, was made manifest.

Abram's father's house worshiped other gods, so naturally, the atmosphere was not ideal for God's glory to manifest. This is confirmed in **Joshua 24:2 (NLT):** ***"Joshua said to the people, "This is what the LORD, the God of Israel, says: Long ago your ancestors, including Terah, the father of Abraham and Nahor, lived beyond the Euphrates River, and they worshiped other gods."*** God is a jealous God, and His first commandment to the Israelites was, ***"You shall have no other gods before me" (Exodus 20:3 AMP).***

God loves His people, but He will not share His glory with another. He wanted to make a covenant with Abram that would last for generations. However, God is subject to His Word, and because He has commanded that we shall not worship any idols or have any other gods beside Him, He certainly could not begin to do what He wanted to do with Abram in his country, amongst a people who served other gods.

What covenant does God want to make with you? What does God want to express through the gate of your life here on the earth? Are you holding up the process because there are idols in your life?

Abram had to make a move both spiritually and physically. Abram's spiritual posture and physical surroundings had to change to host the dimension of the Spirit that God was prepared to pour out – a dimension that would result in the most massive blessing recorded in history, excluding the blessing of Jesus Christ. When Abram obeyed God in faith and was physically and spiritually aligned for God to make a covenant with him, God changed his name to Abraham, which means, 'father of many nations.' His name was changed so that he could embody the expectation of the covenant.

"I will not release a dimension of my Spirit in a place that cannot maintain it." I heard these words in my spirit as this revelation was being downloaded. Wow!

The magnitude of Abraham's covenant was transgenerational. As a result, every family on earth can inherit the blessing of Abraham. There must be a shift in the spiritual for a shift to manifest in the natural, for the natural is birthed from the spiritual. You are your own delay! It is time to move! It is time to go!

Abraham's Strategic Move

God gives the instruction first before He releases the blessing. A 'doing' is required before the release can happen. God can give you an instruction or a prophecy that sounds unbelievable, but because God said it, you know it is possible. However, you must also be obedient to be a partaker of what He wants to do. There is a partnership that must be established. There is a movement that is required from you to become a partner with God. Your participation is indispensable for your God-given destiny to be fulfilled.

You'll never partake of the blessing if you don't partner with the blesser. **~ Dionne Renee ~**

The word 'move' implies action. You must act on the word from God, and there must be some movement from you that shows God you believe what He said and are partnering with Him to bring His word to pass. Abraham became God's partner in his destiny. There are some locations you must leave to better understand the bigger picture of what God wants to do through you. As Abraham moved, God began revealing more of what He would do for Him and His offspring. He began to see what God was showing him. It is evident that Abraham expressed great faith; therefore, He is called a great man of faith. Faith was his strategy. Believing in God and acting on His word was the best decision Abraham made in His life. He looked to the One who is faithful beyond even what words can express. Abraham knew God's faithfulness and understood that God is a man who will bring what He says to pass, so if He made a promise, He is sure to fulfill it.

There is an action that needs to be performed in order to keep God's commands. God does not just go by our agreement in our words; He looks at our hearts, which produce our actions. Words are just mere words if they are not backed by action. Abraham did not only agree with God in mere words, but he moved at God's word. His moving demonstrated his agreement with God's commands and, most importantly, his faith in God's word. He operated by faith at God's instructions because He had experienced the faithful side of God. His faith in God's word provoked him to move.

Hebrews 11:8 (NLT): "It was by faith that Abraham obeyed when God called him to leave home and go to another land that God would give him as his inheritance. He went without knowing where he was going. And even when he reached the land God promised him, he lived there by faith—for he was like a foreigner, living in tents. And so did Isaac and Jacob, who inherited the same promise. Abraham was confidently looking forward to a city with eternal foundations, a city designed and built by God.

Abraham believed God, and so he acted accordingly. Faith is not only believing, but it involves acting, moving, and doing even though you may not see the thing in the natural. It may not make sense, or like Abraham, you may not even know where you are going, but because the command came forth from the reliable One who is faithful until the end, you move. Abraham's faith was because of God's faithfulness to Him. That one attribute of God gave Abraham the ability to possess the faith to move.

I had this dream where I was standing in line at a fast-food restaurant. I was second in the line; however, someone wanted to come and take my place. At the same time, a very tall lady behind the restaurant's counter appeared, called my name, and gave me an instruction. She told me to go and move my vehicle. Without hesitation, I went and moved the vehicle. I knew I would lose my space, however, I still moved. When I moved and reached to the front of the building, I was surprised to see that my vehicle was not what I anticipated it to be. It was a much larger, more luxurious vehicle that was there, and it was mine.

The meaning of the dream was that I would have probably never seen the bigger vehicle if I had not moved when instructed to move. I would not have seen the bigger picture; the enlargement God wanted me to have access to if I had not moved. I probably would have missed it and never received God's blessing.

Bondage Hinders Movement

Just as Abraham was required to move to access his blessing, so were the Israelites. They had to move from Egypt, where they were enslaved, to possess Canaan Land. Their inheritance was not in Egypt, just like Abraham's was not in his father's land.

You will never possess the territory God has shown you until you move from your current location. ~ Dionne Renee ~

God heard the cry of His people and wanted to deliver them from the hands of their slave masters. His promise for them was a land flowing with milk and honey. The land of Canaan was their inheritance, but how could they receive it when they were bound in another country? It's just not possible. It's like you have an inheritance from your parents, yet you are sentenced to prison for 20 years. You will never be able to physically access that inheritance unless you are free from the prison's walls. We can never fully access the possessions God has for us until we are emotionally, mentally, physically & spiritually free. We cannot be bound by the issues of life, demonic spirits, and ungodly mentalities and possess in its fullness all that God has for us. We must move from that place that keeps us in bondage.

***You cannot be a slave to one master and expect to receive blessing from another.* ~ Dionne Renee ~**

CHAPTER 2

Moving Makes Room for Your Gift.

Often, as we see in the reference of Abraham and the Israelites, our shining may not be possible in the place of our birth. This is because our birthplace is a place of comfort, where we have been raised with family and friends and conditioned to a particular environment and lifestyle. What if the solution you carry is for a problem that is many miles away from your homeland? Just thinking about it will make some people shudder in fear because leaving their comfort zone was never an option. Stepping out of our comfort zone is scary, and it tends to make us feel lost and uncertain about what lies ahead. We can observe throughout scripture that once God had an agenda to fulfill on the earth, it was accomplished by any means necessary, even if it meant capturing an entire nation. To further illustrate this, let's look at Daniel, who was a captive in the land of Babylon.

"During the third year of King Jehoiakim's reign in Judah, King

Nebuchadnezzar of Babylon came to Jerusalem and besieged it. The Lord gave him victory over King Jehoiakim of Judah and permitted him to take some of the sacred objects from the Temple of God. So, Nebuchadnezzar took them back to the land of Babylonia and placed them in the treasure-house of his God. Then the King ordered Ashpenaz, his chief of staff, to bring to the palace some of the young men of Judah's royal family and other noble families, who had been brought to Babylon as captives. "Select only strong, healthy, and good-looking young men," he said. "Make sure they are well versed in every branch of learning, are gifted with knowledge and good judgment, and are suited to serve in the royal palace. Train these young men in the language and literature of Babylon" (Daniel 1: 1-3, NLT).

Daniel

With reference to the above scriptures, Daniel was amongst those young men who were taken to Babylon as a captive. The king required that these young men be strong, healthy, and good-looking. They also had to be well-versed in every branch of learning, gifted with knowledge and good judgment, and suited to serve in the royal palace. This indicated that Daniel was already intelligent and wise before he came to Babylon; however, even though he was gifted in these areas, the solution he carried had not been manifested.

His brilliance was not made known in Judah, and his greatness was not seen in his hometown. He never discerned that he had to move from the place of his birth for his shining to be made manifest. In Daniel's case, he was compelled to move because the King of Babylon besieged his country. What he never comprehended was that his moving made room for his rising. What the enemy meant for bad, God turns around for the good of His people. Though the ruthless king's plans were no good, he never would have imagined that one of his captives would become the greatest in his kingdom.

An Excellent Spirit Can Make You a Wonder

God is a God of wonder. He is a statement-making God, and He made a statement with Daniel. God only makes statements of people who will testify of His name and bring glory to Him. If you bring glory to God, He will most definitely bring glory to you. God knew Daniel was faithful, dedicated, and committed to Him. He possessed an excellent spirit and was outstanding in all he did, and because of this, He gained favor with God and man. There will be no favor without diligence, excellence, dedication, and commitment to God and His agenda. There are some things that require the currency of favor; otherwise, there will be no progress.

How you treat the gifts God has given you determines the level of favor you will access. **~ Dionne Renee ~**

Daniel 1:8 (NLT): "But Daniel was determined not to defile himself by eating the food and wine given to them by the King. He asked the chief of staff for permission not to eat these unacceptable foods. Now God had given the chief of staff both respect and affection for Daniel."

Daniel was determined not to defile himself with the king's food, and because of his faithfulness and excellent spirit, God placed favor in the chief eunuch's heart for Daniel. Favor is a currency, and it was necessary for that season of his life. Even though favor with God is fantastic, sometimes it is not enough – we also need man's favor. Remember, anything God does, He does it through the gate called man, so it is vital to gain man's favor, and this is what Daniel was able to do. This favor propelled Daniel to become a wonder.

It is imperative to recognize the currency you need to utilize in your season. **~Dionne Renee ~**

God chose Babylon to be the place where Daniel would thrive and become the star he was destined to be. When God makes a statement, He will do it in the most unlikely places with the most unlikely people. God took a young man and equipped him with divine knowledge, put favor in the hearts of men towards him, and gave him the ability to overcome every challenge he faced, causing him to succeed despite his situation as an exile. God was with Daniel, and it was evident in every aspect of his life.

You Cannot Stay in a Place of Comfort and Do Great Things. Great Things Are Not Found in Familiar Places but in Unfamiliar, Unchartered Territory.

Where your enlargement/inheritance is located is not a place where you will feel comfortable. Daniel had no place of stature in the palace, or so others would have thought, but the call on his life was a palace calling. We know our calling keeps calling us, and in some cases, it pushes and forces us out of the place that is our comfort zone.

Your calling has a location, and sometimes, it may be a location you think is not ideal for you. ~ Dionne Renee ~

If the atmosphere is not correct for your calling, you will never accomplish what you should. If the atmosphere is not calling for the solution you carry, then there will be no manifestation of that solution. If a seed doesn't have sufficient light, water, and vitamins, it will never be able to grow into the great tree it is meant to be. The location and atmosphere must be right, which may require you to move from your current place.

Wisdom Has a Voice

You do not have to say you are wise because the wisdom within you will speak on your behalf. A wise man never has to voice that he is wise; you will see wisdom written all over him. Daniel's gift of interpreting dreams made room for him, as did his intelligence, wisdom, knowledge, and understanding. Wisdom speaks so loudly and forcefully that it leaves an everlasting effect and impact. Thousands of years later, we are still learning from Solomon's wisdom. ***Proverbs 1:20 (KJV): "Wisdom calls aloud outside; She raises her voice in the open squares."***

Wisdom has a voice, and you will know she is present by her actions.

~ Dionne Renee ~

Daniel was made head over the province of Babylon in Nebuchadnezzar's reign. Even after King Nebuchadnezzar passed and King Belshazzar became king, Daniel's wisdom revealed him again. Belshazzar gave a great feast for a thousand of his nobles and drank wine with them. He then gave orders to bring the gold and silver cups that his predecessor Nebuchadnezzar had taken from the temple of Jerusalem. He drank from them with his nobles, wives, and concubines and praised their idols. The gold and silver cups were taken from the house of God and set apart unto Him.

While they were drinking, they saw the fingers of a man's hand appear writing on the plaster of the wall of the king's palace. The king became so afraid he sent for the enchanters and fortune tellers to decode the writing on the wall, for it was written in a language they could not understand. The king offered a reward to the man who could read and understand the writing; however, none of the wise men in his kingdom could read or understand the writing. This made the king even more alarmed and afraid. When the queen heard what was happening, she encouraged the king not to fear, for there was a man with the spirit of the holy gods who could decode the writing. This man was Daniel, and his gift of wisdom preceded him yet again. Your gifts are like magnets in the right location & atmosphere. They will attract jobs, finances, riches, and problems to solve.

***As long as you have developed your gift and make full proof of it, problems that need solutions will find you*. ~ Dionne Renee ~**

Mastery of the Gift Can Bring Deliverance

"The queen, because of the words of the King and his lords, came to the banquet hall. The queen spoke, saying, "O king, live forever! Do not let your thoughts trouble you, nor let your countenance change. There is a man in your kingdom in whom is the Spirit of the Holy God. And in the days of your father, light and understanding and wisdom, like the wisdom of the gods, were found in him; and King Nebuchadnezzar your father—your father the King—made him chief

of the magicians, astrologers, Chaldeans, and soothsayers" (Daniel 5:10-11, NKJV).

The queen described Daniel as one who had the wisdom of the holy gods. When you have mastery, knowledge, and wisdom of the solution you carry, you can be a vessel through which deliverance can flow. As a result of Daniel's gift, the queen was not bothered or even afraid of what was written on the wall, and she encouraged people not to be afraid. She knew about Daniel's wisdom, intelligence, and capabilities, so she had no fear.

Your gift brings confidence to people.

The queen had so much confidence in Daniel that she was adamant that he would be able to solve the problem. Her confidence in Daniel's gift provoked the king to summon Daniel. Being knowledgeable and confident in your gift yields proof-producing results.

The Right Motive for the Gift Causes the Gift to be Subject to You

Daniel 5:13-17 (NLT): "So Daniel was brought in before the King. The King asked him, "Are you Daniel, one of the exiles brought from Judah by my predecessor, King Nebuchadnezzar? I have heard that you have the spirit of the gods within you and that you are filled with insight, understanding, and wisdom. My wise men and enchanters have tried to read the words on the wall and tell me their meaning, but they cannot do it. I am told that you can give interpretations and solve difficult problems. If you can read these words and tell me their meaning, you will be clothed in purple robes of royal honor, and you will have a gold chain placed around your neck. You will become the

third highest ruler in the Kingdom." Daniel answered the King, "Keep your gifts or give them to someone else, but I will tell you what the writing means.

When you completely understand your gift and acknowledge that it is not to be used to obtain riches or fame, that gift promotes you and gives you what you did not even ask for. Daniel's motive for using his gift was to serve and not to abuse what God had given him. He knew that he was a solution provider. Even though the king thought he had to offer Daniel a reward so he could interpret the writings on the wall, Daniel advised him that it was not necessary.

Every person's 'moving' will be different. Some people may need to move from the crowd they usually associate with, while others may have to move from their physical location. Daniel was always studying and developing himself, which shows that moving also has to do with development. Do you think Daniel achieved what he did by staying at the same level? Of course not! Daniel was a man who was always studying, reading, praying, and acquiring the knowledge and wisdom he required. To acquire what God has shown you, you will need to study, develop, and expand your mindset to go to the next level.

Proverbs 18:16 (KJV): "A man's gift makes room for him and bringeth him before great men." God has created you with a treasure on the inside that the world will make room for. You are a solution carrier! You will stand out because of your uniqueness. You become relevant to your generation because of the solution God has placed inside you. Once you have discovered, prepared, and developed the gift, you will begin executing and fulfilling your destiny. Your gift will bring you before great men, and kings shall also come to the brightness of your rising, just like it happened for Daniel.

CHAPTER 3

Shift for Your Miracle

An action is required from you in order to receive your miracle. For space to be made in a furnished room, furniture must be rearranged or moved out, amongst other things. You must make room for your miracle. Making a covenant with God to sow into His agenda makes room for what you reap in your harvest, for when you take care of God's business, He will supernaturally take care of yours.

After many years of taunting from her rival about her barren condition, Hannah finally said in her heart, enough is enough! She not only made a move physically as she stood up, but the move was already made in the spirit. Her mind and heart had already reacted to the discomfort in her spirit even before her body responded. She was in a relaxed position for too long; she had endured Peninnah's insults longer than the desired time. She was in a dormant position and recognized that her circumstances were not changing, so she changed her posture and position.

Do not expect active results if you have an inactive posture.

~ Dionne Renee ~

***Your reality is subject to your moving.* ~ Dionne Renee ~**

***A problem that was discovered at a particular level cannot be solved at the same level.* ~ Dr. Andre Thomas ~**

You must rise to a higher level than where you found the problem; otherwise, there is still a great chance that the problem will conquer you. A higher level is indispensable, and a higher level necessitates a move. You cannot defeat something that is superior to you. Your spiritual condition must change to accommodate your miracle.

Hannah's Strategic Move

1 Samuel 1:3-7 (MSG): "Every year this man went from his hometown up to Shiloh to worship and offer a sacrifice to GOD-of-the-Angel-Armies. Eli and his two sons, Hophni and Phinehas, served as the priests of GOD there. When Elkanah sacrificed, he passed helpings from the sacrificial meal around to his wife Peninnah and all her children, but he always gave an especially generous helping to Hannah because he loved her so much, and because GOD had not given her children. But his rival wife taunted her cruelly, rubbing it in and never letting her forget that GOD had not given her children. This went on year after year. Every time she went to the sanctuary of GOD she could expect to be taunted. Hannah was reduced to tears and had no appetite. Her husband Elkanah said, "Oh, Hannah, why are you crying? Why aren't you eating? And why are you so upset? Am I not of more worth to you than ten sons?" So, Hannah ate. Then she pulled

herself together, slipped away quietly, and entered the sanctuary."

Movement Gets God's Attention

Hannah was tormented by the fact that she could not bear children and by Peninnah's insults and taunts. The situation was so crushing that she had no appetite, and she spent much of her time crying. Did her response to the situation solve the problem or make it leave? Obviously not! It did not cause the issue to cease or disappear; instead, it just became more burdensome. Hannah was like a cripple in the spirit because even after many years had passed, she remained in the same position – crying and defeated. It was as if she just decided to tolerate the situation because she could not see any way out.

Hannah caught God's attention when her spirit woke up from its slumber and moved to a location where God could meet her. Her cry provoked a reaction from God. It was not the type of cry that produced natural tears, but it was a cry that was desperate and hungry for a touch and move from God. It was a cry from Hannah's heart and soul that made the priest think she was intoxicated with strong wine. She made a covenant with God within that cry. She absolutely caught God's attention.

Psalm 34:17 (NASB): "The righteous cry, and the LORD hears, and delivers them out of all their troubles."

I remember hearing a story from a man of God that really caught my attention. He had a daughter that he loved dearly, and while watching her grow, he recognized a particular behavior manifesting in her life. He knew it originated from her genetics, and he understood that if it persisted, it would result in grave ramifications for his daughter. He began to intercede on his daughter's behalf. He fasted and prayed; however, he discerned that he had to move strategically to deal with the problem. One day, while spending time in God's presence, God spoke to him about a particular agenda he wanted him to do. This was when the man of God recognized an opportunity to make a covenant on his daughter's behalf. He did not lapse on this; he moved without delay and went to God. He said, "Father, I heard and understood what you want me to do, and my answer is yes, I will do it, but can you do one thing for me? Can you save and deliver my daughter? If you say yes, I will do your will, and if you say no, I am still going to do your will." With that covenant being made, God answered him and delivered his daughter.

The man of God prayed, fasted, and interceded for his daughter, but he realized that he needed to bring more to the table for the level of the problem he was facing. His cry to God had to capture God's attention and provoke His hand to move. The magnitude of the miracle required more than just a prayer. He had to make a covenant, and that's just what Hannah did. There was no earthly cure for barrenness; therefore, her miracle required a supernatural act of God. She had to access the strange and unusual dimension in God that causes nature to subside, natural protocols to be broken, and the impossible to be made possible. This was the magnitude of Hannah's problem, and it required the supernatural.

You cannot continue to murmur and expect great and awesome results. God's hand will not move for someone who just decides to sit back and take what the world has offered them. Hannah's move was the only thing that caused God's hand to move on her behalf. When you start to move in the spirit from a lower level to a higher one, God will recognize and acknowledge the movement. When Hannah's spirit finally arose, and she realized that her situation was too much for her, she cried out to God, recognizing that He is the Father of Spirits who is omnipotent. She knew it was time to move from the realm of possibility to the realm of impossibility. She moved in faith, and her faith said, "The world says I am barren, but the supernatural says I am the mother of a prophet."

Lack of Movement Causes You to Lose Momentum.

The longer Hannah stood still, the more difficult it became to change her story because as she got older, she was losing momentum. As a result of God's sovereignty, some miracles may have an expiry date. You have no say on how God will perform a miracle. You just need to be in the right posture to receive it.

Move or Miss

Hannah refused to move from where she was and nearly forfeited her miracle. She realized she had to move to receive the solution to her problem. Her cry in the spirit had to change, so she poured her heart out to God at another level.

You can only change your condition by doing something about it.
~ Dionne Renee ~

In order to obtain something, you never had, you got to do something you've never done. ~H. E Ambassador Dr. Andre Thomas ~

If you are not determined to alter your condition, you actually accept it. ~ Dionne Renee ~

1 Samuel 12-16 (MSG): "It so happened that as she continued in

prayer before GOD, Eli was watching her closely. Hannah was praying in her heart, silently. Her lips moved, but no sound was heard. Eli jumped to the conclusion that she was drunk. He approached her and said, "You're drunk! How long do you plan to keep this up? Sober up, woman!" Hannah said, "Oh no, sir—please! I'm a woman brokenhearted. I haven't been drinking. Not a drop of wine or beer. The only thing I've been pouring out is my heart, pouring it out to GOD. Don't for a minute think I'm a bad woman. It's because I'm so desperately unhappy and in such pain that I've stayed here so long."

If you continue to dwell in the place of barrenness, you can only reap what you sow. Hannah moved to pray with such fervor that the priest thought she was drunk with alcohol. She prayed a prayer that was a seed in the spirit for the fruit she wanted to come forth. That prayer was a demonstration of her movement in the spirit realm. As a result of that prayer, she conceived and bore a son. And don't you think the taunting from Peninnah ended as well? Of course, it did!

1 Samuel 17 (MSG): "Eli answered her, "Go in peace. And may the God of Israel give you what you have asked of him." "Think well of me—and pray for me!" she said and went her way. Then she ate heartily, her face radiant."

If Hannah was running a race and was in last place, her position changed after she made that strategic move. That prayer positioned her from being a loser to a winner. It positioned her to receive her miracle, shut her rival's mouth, and brought forth a major prophet to the nation of Israel at that time on the earth. This was the result of her move. From the time she moved, she felt like a different woman; she shifted in the spirit realm. The effects of that shift manifested in the natural – even in her demeanor. Her face became radiant. **(1 Samuel 1:18 NIV: "*...then she went her way and ate something, and her face was no longer downcast* ").**

Inscecurity Hinders Your Destiny from Being Fulfilled

"How long will you succumb to the insults of people?"

"How long will you stay in transit because of the systems of the world?"

"I have given you all power and authority through my Son; why have you not moved with the tools I have given to you?"

"Why are you still standing in the same location?"

These were questions I heard in my spirit that ministered to me. The Holy Spirit was telling me that it was time to make a move spiritually. You can be an enemy to your destiny, and that's what I was faced with at one point in my life. God's agenda for your life will never be small. As a matter of fact, if your purpose doesn't make you feel a bit intimidated, then it is not the entire purpose of God for your life. God will only give you a God-size purpose.

When God revealed to me that I am a Prophetic Psalmist, I tried to believe it with all my heart, but because I could not see it, I did not understand how it would happen. I didn't even have a proper understanding of the word 'prophetic,' and it caused me to doubt. My doubt and insecurity caused me to be spiritually immobile.

How can you doubt the One who created you? However, this happens so many times with so many people. You must see it to have the ability to possess it. God told Abraham, "As far as you can see, that will I give unto you." Seeing was the first principle to Abraham receiving his blessing. Abraham had to see the vision spiritually before he could move towards it.

Genesis 13:14 (NLT): "After Lot had gone, the LORD said to Abram, "Look as far as you can see in every direction—north and south, east, and west. I am giving all this land, as far as you can see, to you and your descendants as a permanent possession."

The first move I had to make was to see what God had revealed to me before I could manifest it. I had to read more and develop my gift; otherwise, it would have laid dormant, and God's purpose for me as a Prophetic Psalmist would never have emerged nor been fulfilled. I am still learning and growing in my gift so my Abba can be pleased, but I had to move. The only way you will climb a staircase is if you move one foot at a time. If you never move those feet to get to the first step, you will never get to the top unless someone takes you there. How can you continue a journey to your destination unless you move?

What you tolerate, you will never change. ~ Dr. Andre Thomas ~

CHAPTER 4

Moving At a Divine Command

When God gives a command, because He is a God of integrity and honors His Word, He will back it. In many instances, we are given a divine command to go here, go there, move now, or stand still, and we do not adhere. When you disobey, ignore, or reject a divine command, negative consequences will follow, and when you adhere to a divine command, you will reap the benefits derived from it.

1 Kings 19:3-7 (MSG): "When Elijah saw how things were, he ran for dear life to Beersheba, far in the south of Judah. He left his young servant there and then went on into the desert another day's journey. He came to a lone broom bush and collapsed in its shade, wanting in the worst way to be done with it all—to just die: "Enough of this, GOD! Take my life—I'm ready to join my ancestors in the grave!" Exhausted, he fell asleep under the lone broom bush. Suddenly an angel shook him awake and said, "Get up and eat!" [6] He looked

around and, to his surprise, right by his head was a loaf of bread baked on some coals and a jug of water. He ate the meal and went back to sleep. [7] The angel of GOD came back, shook him awake again, and said, "Get up and eat some more—you've got a long journey ahead of you."

Elijah's Strategic Move

Elijah was running for his life; he had given up and decided to go under a tree and die. However, after falling asleep, He was awakened by a series of divine commands from God, which he obeyed. At this point, Elijah's spirit was discouraged; however, he was obedient to God's commands.

As he followed the commands, strength returned to his body physically, but strength returned to his spirit first. He was able to make the long journey ahead. Now, remember only moments ago, Elijah wanted to die. He was disheartened and had no hope to go on, but at the voice of the angel, Elijah moved.

A divine command comes with a purpose, and once followed, there is a visible manifestation. ~ Dionne Renee ~

One night, as I slept, I heard in my spirit, "Keep my commands and live." When I finally woke up in the morning, thankfully, I remembered the words, and having the personality that I must search out things, I began to look for those words to see where I could reference them. Soon after, I discovered **Proverbs 7:2,** ***which states, "Keep my commands and live, guard my teachings as the apple of your eye."*** Another Bible version states, **"Obey my commands and live! Guard my instruction as you**

guard your own eyes." I asked in my heart, *Lord, what does this mean*? It sounded self-explanatory, but I still did not really understand the essence of it.

However, months later, I recognized that it was a strategy. God was saying to me, "If you obey my commands and guard my teachings as your own, you will surely live, not just as in being alive, but really live the bountiful life that I have for you. You shall walk in abundance, experience prosperity in every area of your life, and have favor with me and man." I recognized that obedience to God's divine commands is required, and by being obedient, I will experience the type of living God has for me. This made me smile because God was showing me that it was imperative that I obey Him if I wanted to continue this journey of destiny. It is a strategy and a condition required to live an abundant life. Wow, what great counsel I received from those five words (Keep my commands and live),

Subsequently, Elijah was given another divine command. The Lord asked him, "Why are you here?' Elijah answered and gave all the reasons why he was there. God responded to Elijah and said, "Go stand on the mountain at attention before the Lord." And when Elijah obeyed, the Lord passed by him. Some of you may be wondering why God spoke to Elijah and told him to move to a particular location, and He would meet him there. Couldn't God speak to Elijah right where he was?

1 Kings 19:9-11 (NLT): "But the LORD said to him, "What are you doing here, Elijah?" Elijah replied, "I have zealously served the LORD God Almighty. But the people of Israel have broken their

covenant with you, torn down your altars, and killed every one of your prophets. I am the only one left, and now they are trying to kill me, too." "Go out and stand before me on the mountain," the LORD told him."

What God was going to entrust to Elijah required a move, not so much a physical move, but more importantly, a spiritual one. His spirit had to align with what God was about to do. Once his spirit clung to the command, his physical self would automatically obey.

God is a spirit, and He communicates with the spirits of men. He commanded Elijah's spirit to move and get up from that place he was at. That place of depression and discouragement will not attract the agenda God wanted to give him. He had to be in the right frame of mind to anoint the kings that would kill Jezebel. He had to move so that the helper (Elisha) God had appointed for him would be released at the right time. The help that Elijah needed would not have been accessed if he hadn't moved. The solution to saving him from the hands of Jezebel would not have located him if he hadn't moved at the divine command of God.

Can you imagine what would have happened to Elijah if he had not held fast to those commands from God? He would be a dead man. He would have never anointed the kings that brought Jezebel's demise (the person who sought to kill him and who was responsible for placing him in that depressive state of giving up), nor would he have met the helper God was sending him. Worst of all, he would not have made his call an election sure because he would have died under that tree, and his destiny wouldn't have been fulfilled. If he had not moved, he would have never seen that God had already provided the solution to the problem that he was allowing to kill him.

CHAPTER 5

Moving Never Goes Unnoticed

When you continue to stay in a place too long, you take on the characteristics of the atmosphere, and people refer to you according to your environment. According to **Psalm 27:10**, David was rejected by his parents, but he was not referred to at any time as 'David - The Rejected.' He did not allow that place of rejection to be his final residence. He did not make up his bed there because he did not intend to reside in that place. He knew he had to move from that place of rejection. He acknowledged there had to be more to life, and as soon as the opportunity came, he took it and moved.

Moving Can Change a Man-Made Label to a God-Made One

<u>King David</u>

David was known as a man after God's heart because that's where he chose to dwell. He purposed in his heart that he needed to dwell in the secret place of the Most High. In this place, there is no rejection, fear, or depression. Instead, there's the Father and His never-ending love, protection, and immunity from all sickness, disease, and peril. David chose to reside in God's presence. He was a lover of God's presence, so he became what he attracted. He was a great king, a warrior, a worshipper, and an awesome psalmist. Rejection was nowhere to be found around him.

You eventually become a product of what you accept or entertain.
~ Dionne Renee ~

Do you think David would have become the great warrior and king if he had lingered in that location of rejection? Of course not! The very weight of rejection would have caused him to stagger off the course of his destiny. David was the least in his family but refused to stay in that negative place. He was a shepherd boy in the pasture who became one of the greatest kings in the palace. I am sure his unexpected move accompanied jaw-dropping effects for quite a while.

David became the hero of heroes when he slayed Goliath, the Philistine. This was a strategic move that made his influence grow in the nation of Israel. His victory over Goliath caused him to be noticed by King Saul, and it also facilitated his move from a shepherd boy on the pasture to the king's minstrel in the palace, delivering the king from tormenting evil spirits as he played on his harp. God had much to accomplish through David; however, this first move gained him access to the palace. David's process of becoming king required a lot of movement, but he was determined to walk on the path God had set before him.

Jesus Christ

Jesus was born in a stable, and that location alone would suggest he would never be anything great; however, Jesus never once allowed His place of birth to define who He was. He was the Son of God, but He was also the Son of Man with flesh and emotions like any other man. Jesus held onto God's Word and made God's will paramount to His. God's will was His focus, and in everything He did, His focus remained on His Father's business. When He was led into the wilderness to be tempted by the devil, He counteracted each temptation with the Word of God. Jesus understood the power that the Word of God holds. He understood that by meditating on God's Word, the spirit of the very Word would become a part of His atmosphere. He knew that when Heaven became a part of His atmosphere, the presence of God would be with Him, making it even simpler to accomplish His Father's will on earth.

Jabez

1 Chronicles 4:9-10 (NLT): "There was a man named Jabez who was more honorable than any of his brothers. His mother named him Jabez because his birth had been so painful. 10 He was the one who prayed to the God of Israel, "Oh, that you would bless me and expand my territory! Please be with me in all that I do and keep me from all trouble and pain!" And God granted him his request."

There is not much written in the Bible about the man named Jabez. But one thing is for certain: he was born in an environment that harbored pain and sorrow. The circumstances surrounding his life were so dire that when his mother gave birth to him, she called him 'pain.' Can you imagine your mother giving you a name that means pain and sorrow? That was the meaning of his name in the Hebrew language.

What would have caused Jabez to even think of whispering a prayer to Heaven saying, "Oh, that you would bless me, Lord, and enlarge my territory." Knowing his circumstances and what his environment portrayed, he did not allow his location to define who he was. It did not make sense because someone born into that environment would unlikely ask for something of that magnitude. They most likely would be filled with insecurity and have an inferiority complex. Nevertheless, this was not the case for Jabez since he prayed that prayer. He had a different mindset, resulting in him receiving the blessing that He requested from God.

Gideon

Judges 6:12-17, 20-22 (NLT): "The angel of the LORD appeared to him and said, "Mighty hero, the LORD is with you!" "Sir," Gideon replied, "if the LORD is with us, why has all this happened to us? And where are all the miracles our ancestors told us about? Didn't they say, 'The LORD brought us up out of Egypt'? But now the LORD has abandoned us and handed us over to the Midianites."

Then the LORD turned to him and said, "Go with the strength you have, and rescue Israel from the Midianites. I am sending you!" "But Lord," Gideon replied, "how can I rescue Israel? My clan is the weakest in the whole tribe of Manasseh, and I am the least in my entire family!" The LORD said to him, "I will be with you. And you will destroy the Midianites as if you were fighting against one man."

Gideon replied, "If you are truly going to help me, show me a sign to prove that it is really the LORD speaking to me. The angel of God said to him, "Place the meat and the unleavened bread on this rock and pour the broth over it." And Gideon did as he was told. 21 Then the angel of the LORD touched the meat and bread with the tip of the staff in his hand, and fire flamed up from the rock and consumed all he had brought. And the angel of the LORD disappeared. When Gideon realized that it was the angel of the LORD, he cried out, "Oh, Sovereign LORD, I'm doomed! I have seen the angel of the LORD face to face!"

Even though Gideon's design was one of 'A Mighty Man of Valor,' his environment and what he was accustomed to contradicted who he really was. He embraced what man had made known to him all his life, which was 'the least of his clan,' rather than the truth that he was a mighty hero of Israel. It took an encounter and signs from the divine for a drastic transformation in Gideon's mindset to occur. The signs from God shifted him into a whole different person and dimension.

When you move, people may not recognize that you have moved, but they will eventually know that you are not in the same place because movement can never go unnoticed. One of the deep revelations I received about moving is that no matter how silent you are when moving, it is still noticeable. Just as you can see in the natural realm, when a dish is moved from the table to the sink, it is also evident when you move in the spirit.

CHAPTER 6

Knowledge is Indispensable for Any Move

The results we achieve are determined by the knowledge we possess.

~ Dionne Renee ~

We move according to the information we possess. In other words, not having the knowledge of the level or season we are in can limit and hinder us from taking the necessary action. Knowledge gives you the ability to be prepared. When you are prepared, you are more confident because you have the knowledge required for the specific situation or task. You know how to maneuver because of the knowledge you would have received.

For instance, imagine going to New York in December and only packing clothes suitable for summer, oblivious to the fact that it's the winter season. What do you think would happen? This would result in disappointment because you'd be uncomfortable. How can you enjoy your trip if you aren't comfortable? You would also be in danger of freezing to death because of the lack of knowledge about the season.

Lack of knowledge causes limitation, which results in stagnation. But even worse is that you can also become a detriment to yourself. Seasons come, and seasons go. Each season carries its own atmosphere or climate. You must always move or adapt to the necessary season. When a specific season has ended and another season has begun, one must have the ability to discern and move accordingly to suit the season.

This reminded me of when the world was affected by the global pandemic in March 2020, resulting in a great reset. Nations and families suffered great misfortunes. It was a great tragedy socially, economically, mentally, etc. As a result of the pandemic, the way of doing things had to change. Schools, churches, and businesses were all locked down; however, we still had to seek other ways to function adequately enough to maintain a standard of life.

Many people moved with 'the move'. Churches, schools, and many other institutions had to operate via online platforms to fulfill their goals successfully. It was the first time for many children, parents, teachers, and businesspeople to experience working online. Prior to the pandemic, would you have even thought of doing Physical Education online as a subject? Of course not! However, due to the tailspin the world had suffered, everyone, including children, had to move to adapt to this new way of life.

Some businesses, churches, and institutions did not reset or move with 'the move' and have since become relics. Businesses closed because they could no longer operate due to the great losses they had suffered. Some churches closed because they did not maintain their presence, and members moved to other churches that were still relevant because they had an online presence.

All these changes occurred because there was a move, and people refused to move with 'the move.' They tried to continue living life as it had been before the pandemic; however, they were met with immeasurable misfortunes. On the other hand, people, businesses, and institutions that were very aware of the global catastrophe took the information and used it to weigh the pros and cons to move forward successfully.

With the knowledge received and embraced, governments, schools, institutions, and organizations became innovative and took a different posture to survive. This situation reminded me of the wise man who built his house on the rock and the foolish man who built his house on the sand.

Matthew 7:24-27 (NLT): "Anyone who listens to my teaching and follows it is wise, like a person who builds a house on solid rock. Though the rain comes in torrents and the floodwaters rise and the winds beat against that house, it won't collapse because it is built on bedrock. But anyone who hears my teaching and doesn't obey it is foolish, like a person who builds a house on sand. When the rains and floods come and the winds beat against that house, it will collapse with a mighty crash."

We can clearly see how the lack of knowledge can affect movement. Movement is a very crucial part of life, and lack thereof interrupts the divine order of things. Lacking knowledge on a specific subject, agenda, or even your destiny assignment can cause you to be stuck in a place or season longer than you should. Not having the knowledge of what steps to take next or what requirements are needed for a particular task can certainly prevent you from moving forward.

Hosea 4:6 (AMP): "My people are destroyed for lack of knowledge [of My law, where I reveal My will]..."

CHAPTER 7

The Right Mindset is Critical for Moving

Sometimes, we remain stuck or stagnant in places we have outgrown because of our perspective or mindset. Your mindset can be a great hindrance to your moving. It can result in missed opportunities, divine relationships, and connections, and worse, cause you to forfeit your destiny. This brings me to a very popular Bible story about the children of Israel and the land God had prepared for them that was flowing with milk and honey.

Numbers 13:1-3-(NLT): "The LORD now said to Moses, "Send out men to explore the land of Canaan, the land I am giving to the Israelites. Send one leader from each of the twelve ancestral tribes." So Moses did as the LORD commanded him. He sent out twelve men, all tribal leaders of Israel, from their camp in the wilderness of Paran."

Numbers 13:17-20 (NLT): "Moses gave the men these instructions as he sent them out to explore the land: "Go north through the Negev into

the hill country. See what the land is like and find out whether the people living there are strong or weak, few or many. See what kind of land they live in. Is it good or bad? Do their towns have walls, or are they unprotected like open camps? Is the soil fertile or poor? Are there many trees? Do your best to bring back samples of the crops you see." (It happened to be the season for harvesting the first ripe grapes.)"

Numbers 13:25-33 (NLT): "After exploring the land for forty days, the men returned to Moses, Aaron, and the whole community of Israel at Kadesh in the wilderness of Paran. They reported to the whole community what they had seen and showed them the fruit they had taken from the land. This was their report to Moses: "We entered the land you sent us to explore, and it is indeed a bountiful country—a land flowing with milk and honey. Here is the kind of fruit it produces. But the people living there are powerful, and their towns are large and fortified. We even saw giants there, the descendants of Anak! The Amalekites live in the Negev, and the Hittites, Jebusites, and Amorites live in the hill country. The Canaanites live along the coast of the Mediterranean Sea and along the Jordan Valley."

But Caleb tried to quiet the people as they stood before Moses. "Let's go at once to take the land," he said. "We can certainly conquer it!" But the other men who had explored the land with him disagreed. "We can't go up against them! They are stronger than we are!" So, they spread this bad report about the land among the Israelites: "The land we traveled through and explored will devour anyone who goes to live there. All the people we saw were huge. We even saw giants there, the descendants of Anak. Next to them we felt like grasshoppers, and that's

what they thought, too!"

God, the One who knows and sees it all, said to Moses that He was giving the Israelites the land that they were sent to spy on. God is the one who instructed and commanded them to send the scouts out to spy on the land. The Israelites knew of the land because they heard Moses speak about this land time and time again. They knew it was their inheritance from God. So, you would think that after hearing about the land on many occasions, the Israelites would have a different mindset. You would think after the Israelites saw the wonders God had done to rescue and deliver them out of bondage from Egypt, their minds would have been focused on taking the territory that was already theirs. They became distracted by what seemed greater than them because of how they perceived themselves.

They never saw themselves as the chosen generation, the holy nation, or the ones God would thunder down for. They never saw themselves as the ones that God had set apart. They never saw themselves as belonging to the God of all gods who loved them so dearly that He would take on any battle for them. He would smite thousands on their behalf if that's what it took to get them to the destination He had promised to their forefathers.

Never lose focus of what God has spoken or shown you.

~ Dionne Renee ~

Oftentimes, this happens to so many of us as we allow what we see with our natural eyes or feel with our emotions to distract us and cause us to lose focus on what God has promised us. The Israelites were told about this land repeatedly, but it took one bad report to make them forget about the all-powerful God who was backing them all the way. They saw the giants as bigger than the One who opened the Red Sea right before their eyes.

You cannot have a grasshopper mindset and expect to achieve giant results. **~ Dionne Renee ~**

What lives in your mind will become your reality. **~ Dionne Renee ~**

Your thoughts become your reality because they become your focus. Anything that becomes your focus goes from the realm of thoughts to speech and then from speech to action. You are the one who creates your reality by the way you think. Your mindset can stop you from meeting an opportunity that was set up and suited just for you. You can stay in a job longer because you don't think you have what it takes to get another. You can forfeit a destiny relationship because you don't think the person aligns with the vision you had in mind. You can lose out on your destiny because you focus on your emotions and feelings rather than what God told you.

All these examples are the results of having the wrong mindset. The wrong mindset can even thwart your season. Your mindset should always sync or align with your season; otherwise, you will mess it all up. It's the same way with reading a room. You may have gotten into a particular room by favor, but your mindset can get you kicked out. With the right mindset, you become unstoppable. The sky won't be your limit, but your imagination will. Never allow your mindset to become the one thing that causes you to remain stagnant.

CHAPTER 8

From Child of God to Son of God

As a result of Adam and Eve's sin in the Garden of Eden, mankind was lost and in a state of separation from God. Salvation is the solution that God provided for man's sin and separation problem. Salvation is only available through faith in Jesus Christ, believing that He is the Son of God, who died on the cross at Calvary for the sins of mankind. When you repent of your sins and accept Jesus Christ as your Lord and Saviour, the Holy Spirit comes to live inside you, and you become born again and a child of God.

Becoming a child of God is the first phase in your relationship with the Heavenly Father. However, to go deeper in God and access everything He has for you requires moving from child to son. When you are saved, it's your spirit that is saved, and you become a new creation in Christ Jesus because you received a regenerated spirit. However, your body and soul (mind, will, and emotions) are not automatically saved and must go through a process of salvation. This is why you are commanded to work out your own salvation with fear and trembling **(Phil 2:12).** This ongoing process requires a deeper depth of surrender and submission to God.

As you continue to surrender and go deeper in sanctification and crucifying your flesh, there's a movement that occurs in the spirit realm, which transfers to the natural realm. Suddenly, the posture you had as a child of God has developed and moved to the posture of an adult. Just as a caterpillar has its metamorphosis into a butterfly, so is the transformation of a child of God, becoming a son of God.

In the natural, when a child is born, a parent is expected to do things for and take care of the child. It is the same for a child of the spirit. God does things for his children, and He takes the time to guide them by the leading of His Holy Spirit. However, when His children have matured and are now sons, it then becomes not what He can do for them but what He can do through them.

As a son, God is able to express Himself through you because you have now moved to a level where God can trust you to manifest His glory. He can entrust certain tasks to you that He could have never done at the child level. For instance, what father is going to give his 5-year-old son his credit card to go shopping for him? It's the same with our Heavenly Father; He will never entrust delicate things to His children but will only do so to His mature sons.

There are very important aspects of God that you would never experience if you remained at the child stage. Salvation is a very critical stage in one's life. It is the door you need to enter that makes you an heir to God's kingdom. Through this door, you now have access to a spiritual inheritance. However, to receive that inheritance, a lot of movement is necessary.

When Jesus first chose Peter and the other disciples to follow Him, did you think His intention was to leave them how He found them? Of course not! Jesus knew a movement had to happen for Him to do what He needed to do in preparation for His departure from the earth. His church needed to be built on a firm, solid foundation, and He knew that to achieve that, His disciples needed to move to a deeper depth in God's knowledge, wisdom, and understanding. Jesus taught them the Word of God and shared various parables to enlighten their understanding. His teachings brought deliverance, sanctification, and a deeper intimacy with Him. The disciples also learned from Jesus through his actions. When Jesus had completed his task of getting them ready, they were completely transformed individuals. They were no longer just children of God but sons of God. Jesus discovered Peter as a fisherman; however, he was transformed and became a fisher of men who established the church on the earth.

Jesus came into this natural realm we call earth as the son of a carpenter, and He too became a carpenter just like his earthly father, Joseph, but Jesus knew He could not remain as a carpenter. He had to move for the agenda of His Heavenly Father to be fulfilled. He knew His assignment and grew in wisdom to become the person He had to be to host the agenda of God.

As believers, God's desire is for us to move in Him. He wants to take us from child stage to adult/son stage. He wants us to move from drinking milk to eating meat. He wants us to delve into Him and experience Him in His fullness so we can truly live as heirs of His kingdom here on earth. Jesus understood divine principles. He understood that His assignment required more than what He was born with. He did what was required to obtain the necessary results. There is no way that he could have fulfilled his assignment as a carpenter working in a carpenter's shop. Nothing is wrong with being a carpenter; however, for Jesus, it was gravely wrong. If Jesus had remained a carpenter, He would be out of alignment with His Father's will. He needed to rise higher and develop into the prophet, king, savior, and priest He was born to be so that He could fulfill the agenda of God on the earth.

Luke 2:52 (AMP): "And Jesus kept increasing in wisdom and in stature, and in favor with God and men."

The above scripture states that Jesus kept increasing. This just means he kept moving from one level to another. Movement was required mentally, physically, spiritually, and emotionally for Him to access what was necessary in that season of His life. Therefore, Jesus increased in His knowledge and developed an excellent character, resulting in Him accessing favor with God and man. Wisdom and knowledge are required to go from level to level, for the Word of God says in ***Hosea 4:6: "My people are destroyed for lack of knowledge..."***

After Jesus came from the wilderness, where He was tempted by the devil, He went to be baptized by John the Baptist. As He came up from the water when he had baptized, the Spirit of God descended on Him like a dove, and a voice from Heaven said, "This is My beloved Son, in whom I am well pleased." Now, Jesus left Heaven as the Son of God, but isn't it interesting that He was acknowledged by His Heavenly Father when He passed the test in the wilderness and was baptized by John to signal the start of His Heavenly assignment? The Heavenly Father called Him His beloved Son when he moved from a carpenter to His heavenly assignment as mankind's Savior.

I believe that when we move from children to sons in the Kingdom of God, we too can hear, "This is my beloved son, in whom I am well pleased."

CONCLUSION

Moving spiritually and sometimes physically is a very necessary and integral part of fulfilling destiny. In this book, I have outlined some strategies and tools you can use to become an effective mover. As mentioned at the beginning of this book, God is a mover. He establishes His Word, and He acts on His Word. Nothing has ever been accomplished without some sort of motion or movement. Sound was released, and creation came into existence. God spoke, and that sound traveled through the atmosphere and performed what it was sent to do. Sound was meant to move and not to remain stationary.

Stagnation is contrary to the divine order. Remaining stagnant literally interferes with how things are meant to be; therefore, it is abnormal. Everything God creates begins in seed form. God never creates anything in its full maturity, which means that there must be movement. Just as breathing is compulsory to us, so is moving.

Acts 17:28 states that in God, we live**,** ***MOVE***, and have our being; therefore, moving is anticipated by God who created us. It is unacceptable when we do not move because, as children of God, we have His DNA. To be relevant in your generation, you cannot stay still; you must constantly change and move, or as the saying goes, "You must move with the times."

Doctors keep studying and improving so they can possess the knowledge to keep up to date with new techniques, medicine, etc., to be better able to care for their patients. Mechanical Engineers must always be aware of the newest technology and develop their scientific knowledge to design, build, or install new modified components and systems. They are responsible for anything that moves, ensuring that designs function safely and efficiently. They would be failures if they were not constantly moving in their capacity. Can you imagine if both professionals were not continuously moving in accordance with the demands of the world?

Even the very earth we live on moves. Moving is a very integral part of life, whether it's physical, mental, emotional, or spiritual. The Holy Spirit Himself moved upon the face of the earth in the very beginning to create the universe. My absolute prayer is that you grasp the importance of moving and apply the God-given strategies for your life so that our Heavenly Father can be glorified and be pleased with His children.

Made in the USA
Columbia, SC
13 February 2024

31353360R00035